INDIE AUTHOR MAGAZINE

HELLO AND WELCOME!

I'm Indie Annie, and I'm thrilled you're reading this gorgeous full-color version of IAM. Did you know that you can also access all the information, education, and inspiration in our app? It's available on both the iOS App Store and Google Play. And for those that prefer to listen to me read articles, you can pop over to Spotify or our website. Happy Reading!

X

IndieAuthorMagazine.com

Download on the App Store

GET IT ON Google Play

Spotify

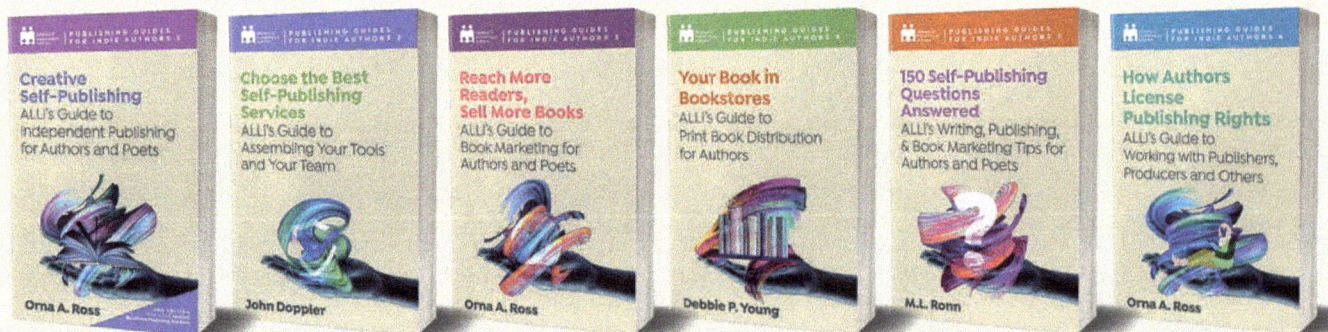

I joined while having a crisis with Amazon KDP... The Alliance is a beacon of light. I recommend that all indie authors join...

Susan Marshall

The Alliance is about standing together.

Joanna Penn

It's the good stuff, all on one place.

Richard Wright

"ALLi has helped me in myriad ways: discounts on services, vetting providers, charting a course to sales success. But more than anything it's a community of friendly, knowledgeable, helpful people."

Beth Duke

See hundreds more testimonials at:
AllianceIndependentAuthors.org/testimonials

IAM

THE FUTURE OF PUBLISHING

Authorpreneurs in Action

"I love Lulu! They've been a fantastic distributor of my paperbacks and an excellent partner as I dive into direct sales. They integrate so smoothly with my personal Shopify store, and their customer support has been top notch."

Katie Cross, katiecrossbooks.com

"Having my own store has given me the freedom to look at my creativity as a profitable business and lifelong career."

Phoebe Garnsworthy, phoebegarnsworthy.com

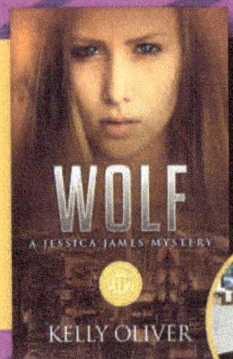

"Lulu has a super handy integration with Shopify. Lulu makes it so easy to sell paperbacks directly to readers."

Kelly Oliver, kellyoliverbooks.com

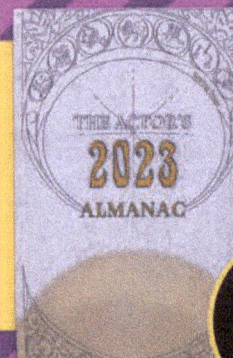

"My experience with Lulu Direct has been more convenient and simple than I anticipated or thought possible. I simply publish, take a step back and allow the well-oiled machine to run itself. Most grateful!"

Molly McGivern, theactorsalmanac.com

INDIE
AUTHOR MAGAZINE

EDITORIAL

Publisher | Chelle Honiker

Editor in Chief | Nicole Schroeder

Creative Director | Alice Briggs

ADVERTISING & MARKETING

Inquiries
Ads@AtheniaCreative.com

Information
https://IndieAuthorMagazine.com/
advertising/

CONTRIBUTORS

Angela Archer, Elaine Bateman, Patricia Carr, Bradley Charbonneau, Honorée Corder, Jackie Dana, Heather Clement Davis, Jamie Davis, Laurel Decher, Fatima Fayez, Gill Fernley, Greg Fishbone, Jen B. Green, Jac Harmon, Marion Hermannsen, Steve Higgs, Chrishaun Keller-Hanna, Kasia Lasinska, Monica Leonelle, Jenn Lessmann, Megan Linski-Fox, Craig Martelle, Angie Martin, Merri Maywether, Kevin McLaughlin, Lasairiona McMaster, Jenn Mitchell, Tanya Nellestein, Russell Nohelty, Susan Odev, Eryka Parker, Tiffany Robinson, Clare Sager, Joe Solari, Becca Syme, David Viergutz

SUBSCRIPTIONS
https://indieauthormagazine.com/subscribe/

HOW TO READ
https://indieauthormagazine.com/how-to-read/

WHEN WRITING MEANS BUSINESS
IndieAuthorMagazine.com

Athenia Creative | 6820 Apus Dr., Sparks, NV, 89436 USA | 775.298.1925

ISSN 2768-7880 (online)–ISSN 2768-7872 (print)

From the EDITOR IN CHIEF

Raise your hand if you're one of those authors who has acted out a scene when they're writing it to make sure it would work. Keep it raised if you've ever mimed a facial expression at your computer screen to help yourself describe it, typed a questionable search into Google while researching for your work-in-progress, made yourself emotional while building to an important moment in your story, or complained about your characters not wanting to cooperate as if they aren't living in your head already.

Check. Check. Check. Check. Check. (That last one happened in my most recent writing session, in fact.)

In the right light, we all probably seem just a little out there. And choosing to be an indie author may just take it a step further. Beyond putting our imaginations to paper in order to make a living, we shoulder the rest of the business responsibilities too. We've chosen to work long hours under looming deadlines, and though our writing communities and avid readers can make our work far less lonely, in the end, most of us can still boast about the expansive collection of hats we wear on our own.

Yet that just makes the support we receive from those closest to us even more meaningful.

For the authors in this month's Mindset article, that support is everything from a cup of coffee delivered to a writing desk each morning, to a partner who delved into the publishing business too. For Malorie and Jill Cooper, who make up the Writing Wives and are featured in this month's cover article, it has been present from the beginning of their story, when they cheered each other on through the "query trenches" of traditional publishing. It may look different for each of us, but it's there in some form, big or small.

It's that support that drives us all forward in this career. It reminds us that, as much as it sometimes can feel otherwise, writing is far from a solo endeavor. And it is a chance to remember that, no matter what—even when we are, maybe, just a little out there—we will always have someone in our corner to cheer us on.

Nicole Schroeder
Editor in Chief
Indie Author Magazine

Nicole Schroeder is a storyteller at heart. As the editor in chief of Indie Author Magazine, she brings nearly a decade of journalism and editorial experience to the publication, delighting in any opportunity to tell true stories and help others do the same. She holds a bachelor's degree from the Missouri School of Journalism and minors in English and Spanish. Her previous work includes editorial roles at local publications, and she's helped edit and produce numerous fiction and nonfiction books, including a Holocaust survivor's memoir, alongside independent publishers. Her own creative writing has been published in national literary magazines. When she's not at her writing desk, Nicole is usually in the saddle, cuddling her guinea pigs, or spending time with family. She loves any excuse to talk about Marvel movies and considers National Novel Writing Month its own holiday.

MARTELLE'S MOTIVATION

Staying Excited as an Author

Is the grind getting you down? The hustle of being an author? It's understandable. In our business, there's always so much to do.

When you feel yourself sinking in too deeply, reach for the convenient vine hanging over the quicksand. What vine? It's the one you put there yourself. It's what got you excited about writing in the first place. It's the thrill of creation. It's the joy of seeing your story come alive when others read it. It's the attraction of money being deposited into your account.

It's realizing the value of your imagination.

Peer groups can be challenging because some authors may find traction more quickly. You'll see them move ahead with substantive careers. Maybe quit the day job. Maybe even buy a new house.

They are not you, and you are not them. Comparison-itis is the thief of joy. You can only be better than yourself from yesterday.

I've written and published nearly two hundred books, yet my latest series didn't take off. It's technically sound, but for whatever reason, it didn't resonate. I'm writing the last book in the six-book series while watching low sales on the first three volumes; four and five are written and waiting to go live. It's hard to get motivated, but you know what lies beyond this volume? Spaceballs! Well, merchandising—that means an omnibus edition, which attracts a different level of reader. It means more opportunities to make money off a finished series, which is marketed differently than a series that's ongoing. It'll be fine. I'll do the best I can writing this last book. I always do the best I can.

And then I'll move on to new stories, ones that are well written and have compelling storylines. I've been outlining ideas the past few months. These are stories I'm jonesing to write.

These are the vines hanging over the quicksand. A series that doesn't sell well won't pull me down. I have a lot more stories to tell. Because that's what keeps me excited about being an author. No one else can tell my stories.

Peace, fellow humans. ∎

Craig Martelle

Craig Martelle

High school Valedictorian enlists in the Marine Corps under a guaranteed tank contract. An inauspicious start that was quickly superseded by excelling in language study. Contract waived, a year at the Defense Language Institute to learn Russian and off to keep my ears on the big red machine during the Soviet years. Earned a four-year degree in two years by majoring in Russian Language. My general staff. career included choice side gigs - UAE, Bahrain, Korea, Russia, and Ukraine.

Major Martelle. I retired from the Marines after a couple years at the embassy in Moscow working arms control issues.

Department of Homeland Security then law school next. I was working for a high-end consulting firm performing business diagnostics, business law, and leadership coaching. For the money they paid me, I was good with that. Just until I wasn't. Then I started writing.

Plottr

Plan Your Books Like a Pro

The Future of Book Outlining is Already Here

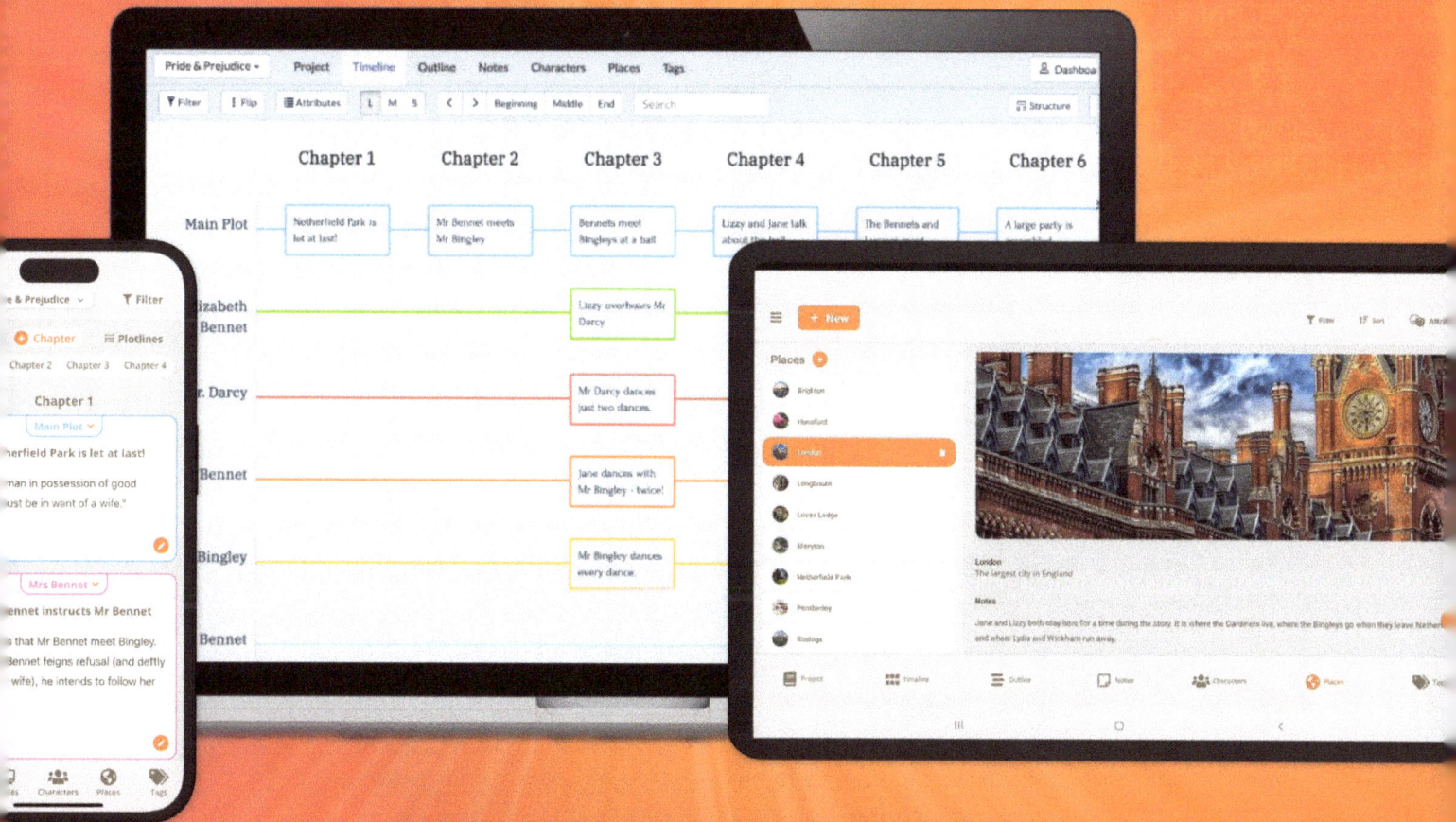

Give the Readers What They Want

What is "writing to market"? The phrase is tossed around a lot in author circles, and especially in independent publishing. The concept involves creating content specifically tailored to what's currently in demand for readers, maximizing the chances of commercial success by writing what readers are actively seeking. You research popular genres, tropes, and themes and follow current trends, such as deciding to write a Post-Apocalyptic Sci-Fi novel because that genre is currently trending. It's an approach that gained popularity in self-publishing circles in part because the quicker timelines in self-publishing allow for a fast response to whatever is currently trending.

Even in traditional publishing, there is often a desire to cling to a bestselling trend and refuse to countenance a genre or topic that does not seem in fashion. When she was first querying, JK Rowling was reportedly told that stories about wizards and magic were not on trend. On the opposite end of the spectrum, as an agented author when *Fifty Shades of Grey* came out, I recall my agent ringing me to see whether I was interested in writing Erotica. I declined, but clearly many authors were coaxed to go that route, as a year later, bookstores were crammed with near-identical covers for near-identical storylines. The difference, of course, is that in traditional publishing, a book will not see the light of day for at least a year and possibly longer. A fast indie author, by contrast, could write and publish a book in a few months.

While writing to market may make it easier to garner sales and reader interest, it can also constrain your creativity and interfere with developing confidence, uniqueness, and authenticity. In this era of global audiences and the internet, niche subjects can still find significant readership, especially when you consider the "long-tail" effect of digital markets—selling fewer products consistently over longer stretches of time rather than selling many volumes of a work at once. Although mainstream bestsellers can get plenty of attention, an array of niche interests have emerged over the past decades, each with their own significant global market. According to the 2023 Indie Author Income Survey, commissioned by the Alliance of Independent Authors (ALLi), authors from the LGBTQIA+ community, some of whom have been rejected by traditional publishing previously for being too niche, were in fact doing extremely well in self-publishing—out-earning straight authors at a difference of 20 percent—because they fully understood their audience and could deliver what they wanted.

PASSION PROJECTS

Connecting with your passion means you're more likely to create engaging, high-quality work that resonates with readers. As generative AI continues to develop, readers are drawn to authors with a human touch and who write with authenticity and passion. Even if a particular subject matter or approach isn't mainstream, it can find sufficient readers to make a living.

Of course, passion alone is not enough. Success also depends on your level of writing skill and publishing skills, and sometimes just on chance. But accessing the power of your passions doesn't just ensure that you enjoy your work and increase your creative energy and capacity; it has practical application in your writing, book production, and marketing, clarifying your options and honing your focus.

By better understanding your own writing passions, you can engage in market research to find out where your passionate readers are. These are the right readers for your work. They have already self-identified and organized themselves in groups that you can access, such as trade magazines, online message boards, social media accounts, hobby groups, and other outlets. Once you can clearly identify your passion, research existing genres and niches that align with your interests. Look for books, authors, and trends that share similarities with your work and help you determine where your book fits within the larger picture.

As you explore the market, think about how you can further refine your book's position. This might involve identifying a specific subgenre or a unique combination of elements that distinguishes your work from others. You can also, in becoming better aware of what a particular readership enjoys, lean into their preferences from your own passions. Do readers of Regency Romance prefer a duke to an earl? Consider promoting your hero to a higher rank. Do nonfiction readers like case studies? Then include those in your book. Do children's books with an associated activity included at the end fly off the shelves? Then help those parents. Knowing that a series is likely to sell better than a stand-alone book does not mean you should never write another stand-alone, but you could spend an extra hour of your time considering whether there is scope for developing a series. Knowing your passions and understanding the market and your place in it is a winning combination.

A couple of interesting exercises and a thought-provoking podcast episode to leave you with:

What do you love? If you're a newer author, reflect on what most excites you about your own writing and the books you most love to read. What do they have in common? If you're like most people, you have several passions reflected in your reading and writing. What do you most enjoy reading and writing about, under the four headings of theme, character type, setting, and style?

What do your readers love about you? For established authors, spend a little time reading your best reviews. What do your readers most often mention? Try making a word cloud of their reviews to see what emerges; the results may offer new insight into what your readers hope to find in future works.

Use your creative passion to discover your niche. In the May 21, 2023, episode of the *Creative Self-Publishing Podcast*, ALLi founder and Director Orna Ross discusses using your creative passion to discover your genre, niche, and micro-niche with podcast producer Howard Lovy. Listen to it at: https://selfpublishingadvice.org/creative-passion. ∎

Melissa Addey, ALLi Campaigns Manager

Melissa Addey, ALLI's Campaign Manager

The Alliance of Independent Authors (ALLi) is a global membership association for self-publishing authors. A non-profit, our mission is ethics and excellence in self-publishing. Everyone on our team is a working indie author and we offer advice and advocacy for self-publishing authors within the literary, publishing and creative industries around the world. www.allianceindependentauthors.org

Dear Indie Annie,

My biggest obstacle in my career is profitability. I have a full series of eight books, with great read-through. I do everything I'm supposed to do to advertise them: Facebook Ads, freebies, group promos, daily posts on social media. But I'm still not earning much. How do I make money in this business?

Seeking More Sales (Aren't We All?)

Dearest Seeking Sales,

Oh, my little crumpet, this profit pickle has so many of us in a jam! But never fear—with a spot of shrewd marketing and a pinch of perseverance, I can see some serious sauce streaming your way.

First, we must get to the meat of the matter. Are your titles tasty to readers, or is the recipe a bit stale? Analyze those reviews like Gordon Ramsay studies a soufflé. Any constructive criticism on improving your batter, love? Does the plot need more flavor? Do tensions fall flat? Don't be afraid to rework weak elements. Even renowned chefs adjust recipes until they're Michelin-worthy!

Might I suggest you invest in Theodora Taylor's *7 FIGURE FICTION: How to Use Universal Fantasy to SELL Your Books to ANYONE (Universal Fantasy™: Butter Up Your Writing)*? In between her yellow covers, you will find out about the importance of "butter" in fiction, and as any French chef will tell you, butter is key.

Once your book is delicious, how do you get it out there for your hungry readers to devour? You said you are already doing all the things; well, do them again and again and again. Promote via multi-author Facebook

Groups, choose targeted hashtags on Instagram that fit your genre and vibe, and collaborate with authors in your niche for giveaways. Partnering expands your reach immensely. Solo shouting into the void goes unheard! And if you aren't on TikTok and using the sensation that is #BookTok, then get your TikTok game on, especially if your potential audience is young, hip, and happening. Reread past copies of *IAM* for lots of great advice on how to freshen up your social media and advertising.

Patience and persistence are

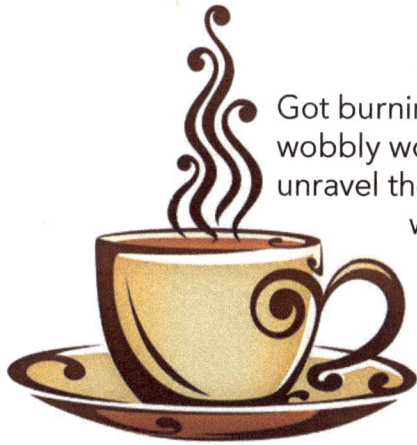

Got burning questions about the wibbly-wobbly world of indie authoring? Eager to unravel the mysteries of publishing, writing woes, or anything in between? Give your quizzical quills a whirl and shoot your musings over to indieannie@ indieauthormagazine.com. Your inky quandaries are my cup of tea!

the secret herbs and spices, darling one. As Hemingway said, "There is nothing to writing. All you do is sit down at a typewriter and bleed." Keep grinding; sales will come, my little chocolate gateau. Consistency pays off. Master marketing with guides like Joanna Penn's *How to Market a Book* or Ricardo Fayet's *How to Market a Book: Overperform in a Crowded Market*. Let their wisdom season your strategy.

Track precisely where sales originate. Analytics tools like Publisher Rocket or Book Brush identify your "superfans." Tailor ads and promos to those groups. Study reviews to see what draws readers in. More Romance than Fantasy? More action, less cozy? Adjust your recipe! As Twain said, "Many a small thing has been made large by the right kind of advertising."

And finally, don't forget the importance of a good cover and book description. You mentioned you get good read-through, so increased sales are possible once you get readers to taste your wares. Remember, we eat with our eyes first, so are your books whetting their appetites? Ask other authors in your

genres, or even ask your readers through your newsletter, to critically appraise your covers. Take a forensic lens to the top-selling books in your genre. How do yours sit alongside them? Do your covers draw readers in, and do your blurbs make their mouths water? Fixing your blurb is quick and free to do. The covers may take more time and money, but this investment will be worth it. Use only the choicest ingredients if you want to be the best.

This is a seven-course marketing meal, not a snack. Stay open to feedback, keep passion kindled, constantly improve your book "ingredients," and your sales will flourish! Now onward, my petite pastry chef. That bestseller dough won't knead itself.

Bon appétit!

Happy writing,
Indie Annie
X

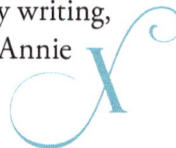

10 TIPS FOR

BATCH-CREATING CONTENT

Content creation for social media can be fun and engaging, but it can also be time consuming and tedious. Batching content creation—focusing on one step in the creation process for several projects at once rather than finishing one project before moving to the next—reduces task switching and saves you time and brain power as you create. Each batching session can result in many pieces of content, which you can then schedule over a longer period. With the right process, you could get an entire year of content ready to go.

How? Read on for *IAM*'s top tips for creating social content in batches and saving yourself time and effort in the long term.

1 IDENTIFY YOUR IDEAL READER.

As you build your social media, imagine your books' perfect reader and the traits or characteristics they may have. Not all your readers will fit this exact ideal reader demographic, but the better you can tailor your content to a specific group or subset of people, the more likely you are to find your audience and the people who will read, buy, and love your work. Think in broad categories, such as age range, but also consider other books and fandoms they will likely enjoy, and pull from those.

2 CREATE 'BUCKETS' TO SORT YOUR SOCIAL POSTS.

Choose a couple of main content categories to direct the content you're going to create. What are your brand values? What has been popular in the past, and what is currently trending? What would your ideal reader like to see? Helping to solve a problem or giving people something to relate to will make followers more likely to interact with your content. Focus on broad umbrella categories, like a love of books. This might also be your genre or a smaller subset of your genre. Choose three or four big buckets that fit your brand, that you have an interest in, and that are something that will interest your ideal reader. Finding and analyzing comparable authors can help you narrow your focus here as well, since your readers will likely overlap.

3 NARROW YOUR FOCUS FURTHER.

Break the larger umbrella categories down until you get a couple of subcategories in each. This is one way to get ideas for an entire year at once—if you end up with a couple of smaller buckets for each of your larger ones, you could have twelve in total, which works out to one focus idea for each month. This keeps your content fresh and helps you stay on target. Under the more general books bucket, some options are offering tips for managing or lamenting the infamous TBR (To Be Read) list, page flips with synopses and/or tropes for your books, and a series of photos or character art that flash on the screen to music. Trending sounds relating to books are another option, but hopping on the trend in time might mean scheduling within a shorter time frame.

4 GENERATE PROMPT IDEAS.

Start brainstorming specific posts related to each of your smaller buckets—ideally about thirty for each, if your account is planning a post once a day. Here's where internet searches and AI can be helpful. Prompting something like, "List 30 questions for Fantasy book readers" will get you started. Questions are good to get engagement from your viewers, and paying attention to what is trending can help you create the kinds of posts the social media algorithm is more likely to promote. You want to mix it up so the content doesn't feel repetitive, but you also don't need to have each day be wildly different.

Pro Tip: Only a small percentage of your followers are likely to be shown your content on social media sites, so you can recycle some key posts, especially those that generated a big response.

5 KEEP YOUR WORK ORGANIZED WITH SPREADSHEETS.

Put your content into a spreadsheet to make uploading easier. Canva Pro, for example, allows bulk uploads from a spreadsheet. You could generate several prompts at once, put them into a spreadsheet, and then, using the "Bulk Create" tab, get your prompts into usable content based on templates you've set up beforehand. You can keep a running list of hashtags in a spreadsheet or a list of the best quotes or hooks from your books. Spreadsheets can also be used as a scheduling calendar, including dates and scheduling for different social media accounts.

6 STAY ON THEME.

Come up with a theme and build some templates to use while you're working in your graphic design software. This can keep your author brand consistent and help your readers recognize it, and if it's a meme or something shareable, putting your own name on it can help get eyes back on the original content even if it gets shared without attribution. Plus, having something that is branded and ready to go will help you create more content on the fly.

7 BUILD A B-ROLL LIBRARY.

You don't have to film new footage for each short video you create. Of course, if you are doing something with prompts or dances, you might need to break out the camera, but for other posts, find some simple posing ideas and record those. For example, standing along the side of the frame against a plain wall while looking to the side, where you can add text in post-production, can be used in many ways. If you analyze other creators, you will see that this less active content is put in with the more labor-intensive content to mix it up. Batch-filming also might mean a shirt change or coming up with a new background, or perhaps using the same background as a theme in videos and looking in different areas or using simple movements. With the right editing and text, these simple photos and videos can be repurposed for new content.

8   SPEND TIME IN THE SOCIAL MEDIA SPACE WHERE YOU WANT TO WORK.

If you interact with other authors, especially similar and popular authors, as well as book-related influencers and readers, you can see what's current in the zeitgeist and pick up on trends to add to your ideas list. You can also respond to your comments and interact with other accounts to show interest and make new connections.

Pro Tip: While you are scrolling, don't forget to use the "save" feature. This is where you can find sounds you want to use, save videos you want to share, or mark an example of a trend you can redo with your own twist. Let your fellow creators inspire you!

9   ADD THE FINAL TOUCHES.

Once you have everything filmed or your prompts generated, it's time to go into post-production. This part can be time consuming; however, batching it will help you get through more than doing one at a time would. This is when you can reuse those longer poses you just filmed and make several with different wording. Your hashtag spreadsheet will enable you to copy and paste the best hashtags for your content. A spreadsheet with quotes, hooks, tropes, and memorable scenes from each book can help you figure the best text to include. Add in music or sounds, and don't forget trending sounds, if you can post quickly enough to jump on those trends. Post-production is also when you focus on transitions and the smaller details—but remember, progress over perfection.

10   SCHEDULE YOUR CONTENT.

Some platforms have a built-in planner or scheduler, but there are several apps and software that will allow you to do this ahead of time and use their more specialized features, like auto-scheduling based on when your audience is most active or scheduling your content several months ahead in one sitting. Then you have more time to scroll and interact with your followers—or even get your words written for the day. ∎

Jennifer Green

Jen B Green

Jen B. Green has lived in five countries on four continents with her three sons, two daughters, and one great guy. She reads anything that stays still long enough, plays piano, and bakes everything sweet.

After earning her Ph.D. in psychology, Jen tried writing a novel for Nanowrimo and was hooked! Her days are spent traveling the world, teaching undergraduate psychology, and wrangling her growing homemade army, but her nights are for writing Urban Fantasy with witches and werewolves.

PLANNING TRAVEL TO A CONFERENCE?

Use miles.

Explore ways to make the most of your award miles.

Writelink.to/unitedair

Wives' Tale

AS THE WRITING WIVES, MALORIE AND JILL COOPER MAKE MARKETING SUCCESS ACCESSIBLE TO INDIE AUTHORS

When asked about the advice they would offer indie authors heading into a new year, Malorie and Jill Cooper start their answers at the same time.

"You go first, Mal," Jill tells her wife with a laugh.

"I figure we're probably going to say the same thing, actually," Malorie says.

In the end, Malorie is right. It doesn't matter who answers first, or that they're speaking from separate rooms of their house: Malorie from the sunroom and Jill from the basement. As they have been for much of the interview, the literary couple—both authors themselves and co-founders of the marketing agency The Writing Wives—are on exactly the same page.

For roughly the past five years, Malorie and Jill have offered classes and one-on-one mentorships to authors looking to run Facebook Ads for their businesses after mastering the platform themselves. In addition, the two have written and published more than one hundred fifty books between them since entering the indie author sphere in 2011, earning bestseller monikers from the *New York Times* and *USA TODAY*, respectively. For all their eye-opening successes, however, the message of the Writing Wives' story remains grounded. Ultimately, their careers have been shaped by the idea of finding a balance between writing and real life—and by the desire to support each other, and others in the community, when that balance starts to tip.

PASSIONATE PURSUIT

Fittingly, the Writing Wives' story begins with writing. Malorie and Jill met in a writing chatroom in 1996 and later married. For years, they encouraged each other as they worked to find a traditional publisher for their respective projects.

"Back then, I only wrote passion projects," Jill says. "I didn't know anything else. Writing to market wasn't a thing. You just wrote what you loved." So when an agent said the manuscript she'd been querying showed promise, she was thrilled—but when he reviewed the project further and turned it down, his rejection stung that much more. "That's when I saw, on Twitter, some of my friends were publishing. From looking outside, it looked like they were doing really well, and … I was like, 'I want to do that too.'"

Malorie's experience with the process was similar—her hope was piqued when an agent requested her full manuscript, then dashed when six months went by without a word. It wasn't until she reached out for a follow-up that she learned it was another rejection. The two finally made the

The Writing Wives

Indie author marketing group

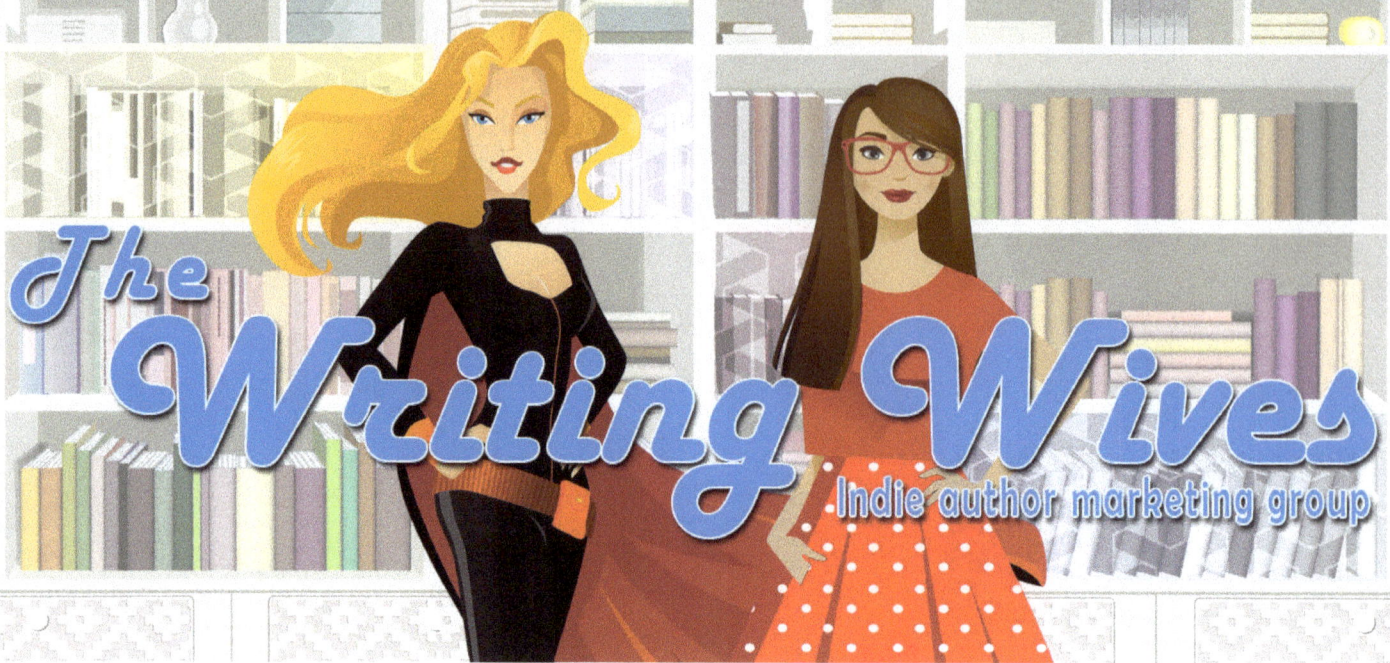

shift toward independent publishing in 2011, but in a corner of the industry that was just finding its footing, that posed its own challenges. The two had to find editors, learn interior formatting, and hire someone to organize book blog tours to promote their work. In addition, Jill had to find a cover designer for hire; Malorie decided to create her own.

"We didn't know what we didn't know," Malorie says.

As time went on and the community around independent publishing grew, however, Malorie and Jill saw their author careers grow too—thanks, in part, to advertising on Facebook. Malorie's books sold especially well, and by 2017, they were earning enough for her to transition to writing full time.

"I said to Jill, 'I'm really inspired right now,'" Malorie says. "'The sales are really good, but we've seen so many authors who started this years ago and just don't write at all anymore. You know, they had careers and they got burned out, or Amazon changed something, and the way they're making money stopped working. So let's make hay while the sun's up.'" The couple agreed Malorie would take the next year to write as much as she could and develop her backlist, with Jill supporting her.

By the end of 2018, Malorie had published forty-four books—and, as she says, "completely destroyed my desire to write."

"I was watching you," Jill says to Malorie. "The words were slowing down, and the inspiration—the well was dry." By 2020, the couple decided they needed to find a way to give Malorie a chance to rest and recharge. Malorie briefly considered returning to her day job as a software engineer; instead, the wives started offering classes on Facebook Ads for authors.

THE WRITING WIVES

Although the COVID-19 pandemic slowed the couple's start, as people slowly returned to status quo, the handful of classes the two were hosting grew into a full-time business. Today, the Writing Wives offers a mix of marketing classes at a variety of skill levels and individual consulting, all still focused on Facebook Ads. The process has been a learning experience for more than just its clients.

"I think the biggest struggle that I've had myself that Jill's really helped me through is [that] … my biggest fear is failing to teach people and help people," Malorie says. "At the very beginning, I refused to charge any meaningful amount of money for anything because I figured at least if I'm terrible, they'll be like, 'Well, it wasn't that much.'"

Confidence can be a major drawback for the couple's students as well, Jill says. Some authors get nervous about investing the money and time in their marketing to see success, and others want to build a marketing campaign for one or two books instead of waiting to build a backlist first. As much as the couple hopes to teach authors how to master Facebook Ads, they also want to support them in the process.

"My mission statement is to make Facebook Ads accessible to all authors," Jill says. And for all the support they've offered indie authors through the Writing Wives, they've received just as much support from the community in turn. Around the same time they settled on a name for their business, Malorie came out publicly as transgender. "Ironically, the least accepting part of the community was the genre I write in, which is Science Fiction. And specifically I read Military Science Fiction. So I lost a lot of friends in that group. But at the same time, I made so many more friends in the community," she says. "I can't think of any community I've ever been in that is as open and welcoming as the author community."

WORDS OF ADVICE

Looking ahead at 2024, Malorie's biggest piece of advice for authors—and Jill's, it turns out—is to pace yourself. "Remember that you also want to have a life," she says. "Like Jill said, even if you can write five thousand words a day, you can't write five thousand words a day for 365 days. You're going to get sick. You're going to want to spend time with the kids."

"Don't run yourself ragged, authors," Jill says. "Take care of yourself. Be with your family. Learn how to make the most out of what you've already written, and use it as more than one revenue stream to relieve some of that pressure so you don't have to burn yourself out completely."

At the same time, Jill says, remember that you're a business owner, and many of the roles you take on as an author require a business mindset—including marketing. Sometimes, success comes from being able to step back from your creative goals and look at them from an outside perspective. "And if you get your spouse on board to be that other person, that can also work in your favor," she says with a smile. ∎

Nicole Schroeder

Nicole Schroeder

Nicole Schroeder is a storyteller at heart. She holds a bachelor's degree from the Missouri School of Journalism and minors in English and Spanish. Her previous work includes editorial roles at local publications, and she's helped edit and produce numerous fiction and nonfiction books, including a Holocaust survivor's memoir, alongside independent publishers. Her own creative writing has been published in national literary magazines. When she's not at her writing desk, Nicole is usually in the saddle, cuddling her guinea pigs, or spending time with family. She loves any excuse to talk about Marvel movies and considers National Novel Writing Month its own holiday.

Name Your Price

DO AUTHORS' IDEAL PRICING STRATEGIES VARY BY THE GENRE THEY WRITE?

Most pricing strategists tell indie authors to write in a genre that sells well and price competitively. But for new authors and those switching genres, choosing how to price your book may not feel that simple. Factors like publishing goals, format, email list size, series placement, KU status, market research, and perceived value all play a role in selecting an effective price for your book. One way to filter your options is to apply these factors through the lens of genre.

Genre expectations already account for the average length of a book, as well as various levels of formatting. Science Fiction and Fantasy, for example, are often longer than Romance novels and are more likely to offer special edition hardbacks with additional artwork, maps, or sprayed edges. Readers anticipate a higher price when the packaging of the story is more complicated.

Looking at the pricing for similar books in your genre can help determine a range of prices to apply to your own work. From there, you can choose something in the higher or lower range, depending on your specific goals. A first-in-series might be priced lower to act as a magnet for other books in your backlist. If you already have a large email list of dedicated fans, you might choose to price your book higher to meet the perceived value of your work.

Bestselling Romance novelist Jillian Dodd says, "Indie authors with great covers and a proven track record should be pricing at similar prices to trad [traditionally] published books in their genre."

Likewise, author and *IAM* contributor Chrishaun Keller adds, "Price is not an indicator of quality, but we as readers do wonder if the publisher has confidence in a book that comes out the gate at a price lower than I'm used to paying."

IngramSpark, Draft2Digital and Amazon KDP all provide guidance on pricing for their authors, but their recommendations may seem too broad to be useful. Marketing and market research tools like Publisher Rocket, KDSPY, and Kindletrends can help identify an appropriate range for your genre. Dave Chesson discusses using Publisher Rocket to price e-books on Kindlepreneur. C.S. Lakin reviewed KDSPY for TheSelfPublisher.com, and Nat Connors provides detailed market research through his Kindletrends newsletter.

In a recent newsletter, Connors looked at trends within the top one hundred Kindle e-books for three genres. According to his research, nearly 80 percent of Fantasy e-books on this list sold above $3.99. Romance shows a similar price breakdown, though Fantasy had a higher percentage of books above $4.99. Almost 40 percent of Mystery, Thriller, and Suspense books on the top one hundred list are priced at or below $3.99, with more $0.99 books than either of the other major genre categories compared.

FANTASY

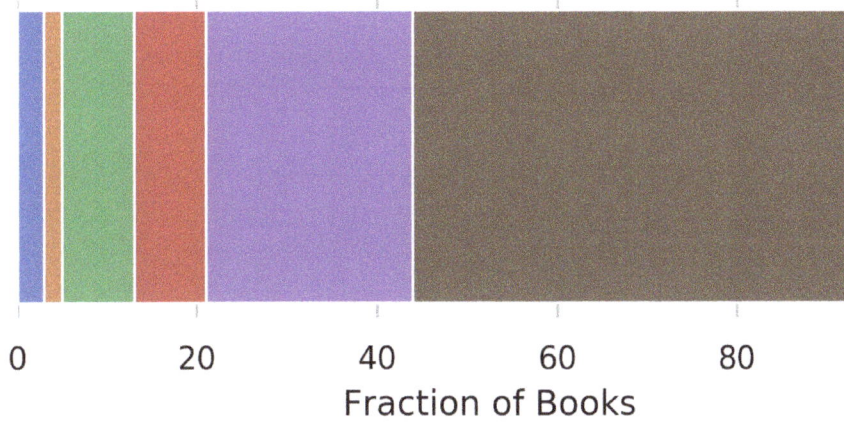

Fraction of Books

ROMANCE

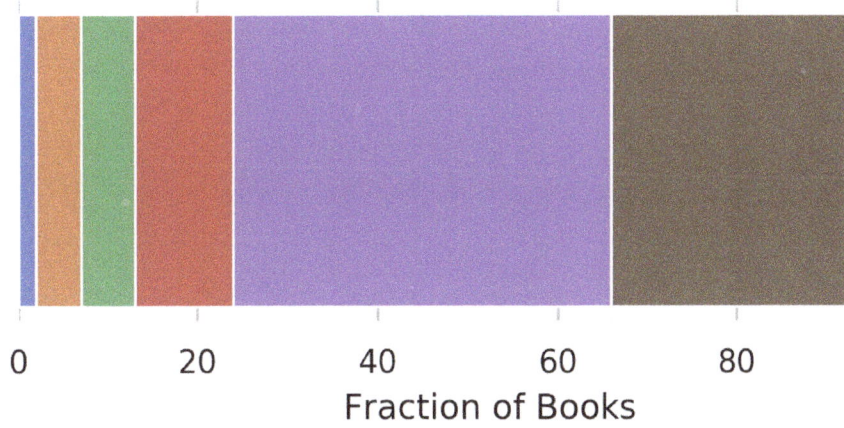

Fraction of Books

MYSTERY/THRILLER/SUSPENSE

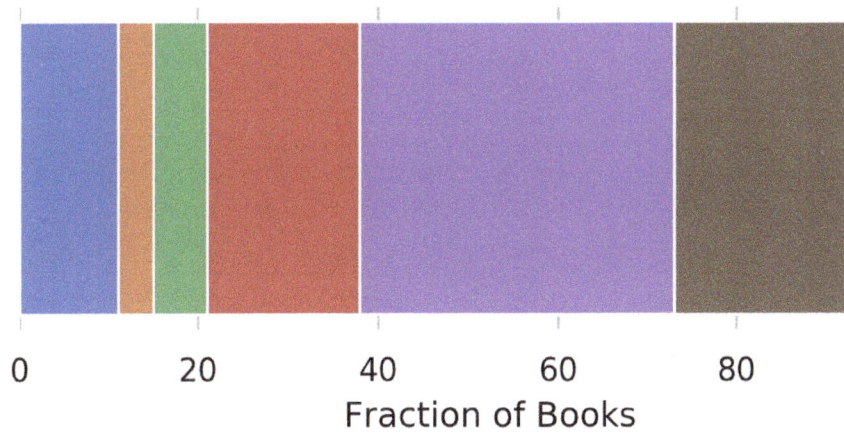

Fraction of Books

Here's how some indie authors use genre expectations to determine pricing for their books.

GENRE AS A STRICT GUIDELINE

Bree Moore, who writes Urban, Paranormal, and Epic Fantasy, says, "I park mine right in the middle of other indie authors in my genre, though I've started to raise it [prices] a bit more." She says she "had a desire to see what my audience would tolerate. So many e-books, especially trad published, are priced $10 to $20. I figured I might be selling myself short." So far, the increase in price has not affected her sales numbers.

Beck Grey is the author of five LGBTQ+ Contemporary Romance books, published in e-book, paperback, and audiobook formats. When pricing for retailers, Grey's first goal is to look at "the leaders in my genre and check out what they price their books for," Grey says. "Then I usually go with the average for pricing on mainstream retailers." The author's direct pricing strategy for paperbacks is similar, with an added discount to account for the cost of media mail "since many people have Amazon Prime so get free shipping."

Horror and Paranormal Comedy author Scott Burtness has been publishing "on and off for ten years." He says he started out pricing his books among lower comps but has shifted prices up and down over the years while staying with genre expectations, which tend to be lower due to the shorter average length of Horror and Paranormal Comedy books. "What I found interesting was that when my books were at $0.99 or $1.99, I didn't sell as many units. When I put the price up to $2.99 or $3.99, I sold more units. But once I hit $4.99, orders went down again."

GENRE AS A PIECE OF THE PUZZLE

Lisa Cassidy writes Epic Fantasy for both adult and YA audiences. While she primarily focuses on pricing within genre expectations, she says she also considers "those that are close in content/tone, etc. to mine that are doing well (i.e., ranking in Top 100 lists)." She reviews these price comparisons

"every twelve months or so" and adjusts accordingly, usually increasing her prices to match the market.

William Brinkman prices his Sci-Fi and Urban Fantasy according to genre but leaves some room for promotions. "Currently, I have one permafree book, which is a short story collection. I use it as an introduction to the series, and it's too short for me to justify charging for it. The novelette I charge $2.99 for so I can run sales for $0.99 later on. The novel is at $3.99, and I can occasionally run $0.99 specials. I've also tried to survey Urban Fantasy book prices using Publisher Rocket, K-lytics, and by eyeballing the Amazon charts. So it's a matter of trying to stay within genre expectations and allow room for occasional sales."

Women's Fiction and Suspense author Pamela Kelley says, "I price according to genre but also by how long I've been doing this and size of readership. I only recently bumped from $4.99 to $5.99 and was nervous about doing so. When I first started in the genre I priced at $3.99 to make it more of an impulse buy—and that worked well."

PRICING WITHOUT CONSIDERING GENRE

Spicy Romance author Emilia Rose says she "used to price based on genre, but I've since stopped." Now her pricing strategy "varies from platform to platform." Having come from publishing on Wattpad to now running six-figure subscriptions on Ream and publishing her e-books through KDP, she wants "to be as accessible to readers as possible because it's important to me for lower income readers to be able to read my books." To that end, she still offers her rough drafts free and has made her e-books available through libraries. When she publishes her final copies through retailers, however, she asks a higher-than-average price for her genre. Since readers who can't afford this increase have other ways to access her content, she says, "my readers have not reacted negatively."

Clint Chico, a high school teacher writing Contemporary YA novels that feature LGBTQ+ characters, also tries to keep his books at a price point his young readers can afford. He tends to consider length over genre: "KDP requires that you charge enough to cover printing costs, and my books range between 70,000 words and 150,000 words (250-450 pages). So most of my paperbacks have to cost $9 or more." His e-books are priced lower than genre averages and are enrolled in Kindle Select. "I don't see Horror or Romance costing any more or less than Fantasy or Sci-Fi, so I'm not pricing my books any differently according to genre."

Pricing your book can be daunting, but it doesn't have to be a permanent decision—and probably shouldn't be. Book prices fluctuate regularly as authors consider their goals, seasonal sales shifts, promo opportunities, and other factors. As your experience grows and the market changes, take some time to reevaluate where your book fits into your overall author business plan. Then measure the weight of those other factors.

Authors are often encouraged to consider genre norms when writing for publication, and even if they aren't writing to market, most authors consider reader expectations as part of their business plan. Including genre trends in your pricing strategy might be a good first step, especially for emerging writers. ◼

Jenn Lessmann

Jenn Lessmann

Jenn Lessmann is the author of Unmagical: a Witchy Mystery and three stories on Kindle Vella. A former barista, stage manager, and high school English teacher with advanced degrees from impressive colleges, she continues to drink excessive amounts of caffeine, stay up later than is absolutely necessary, and read three or four books at a time. Jenn is currently studying witchcraft and the craft of writing, and giggling internally whenever they intersect. She writes snarky paranormal fantasy for new adults whenever her dog will allow it.

Tax Prep for Indie Authors—
It's Not as Scary as You Think!

Tax season is rapidly approaching for those of us in the US, and whether you're full-time or just starting to see sales, if you made money from your books last year, it has the potential to be complicated. Although we're not qualified to give direct financial advice regarding paying taxes as an indie author, *IAM* has a few tips about preparing for tax season that should help anyone who needs to pay taxes in the US this year. In this article, we'll touch on the forms and paperwork you need to compile, applicable deadlines, and some additional tips to make the process flow as smoothly as possible.

Note: If you live outside the US, your country's tax laws and requirements likely differ from those described in this article. Additionally, the following information cannot be considered direct financial advice and is meant for general education purposes only. For advice and information regarding your specific financial situation, contact a CPA or accountant who understands the federal and state laws that will apply to you.

KNOW YOUR ENTITY

One of the most important factors to understand as you prepare for tax season is your business structure—how your taxable income flows through to your personal tax return. If you haven't legally filed to become an LLC, a partnership, an S corporation, or a C corporation, then you'll be filing as a sole proprietor. For more on LLCs, read guest author Joe Solari's breakdown of various business structures from the October 2022 issue.

Even if you have a regular job collecting a W-2, you'll need to file additional income from your author business with a Schedule C form. For federal taxes, this applies universally, but each state may have additional requirements. Hiring a professional firm or individual tax professional or purchasing a highly rated, reputable tax software can help guide you through the intricacies of dealing with the IRS. In the long run, ensuring that all your i's are dotted and t's are crossed is worth the peace of mind that comes with properly satisfying your tax liabilities.

Sole proprietor:
As a sole proprietor, you will use Schedule C to report business income and expenses. You are responsible for paying self-employment taxes, including Social Security and Medicare.

Partnerships and corporations:
Partnerships and corporations are typically set up with the assistance of a business or tax attorney. If this is a step you've taken, then that professional should also assist with tax preparation and filing or should recommend another professional to assist you.

- **Partnerships:** A partnership must file an information return but typically does not pay federal income tax. If you have a business partner, you will likely file as a partnership or corporation and use an information return to report certain business transactions to the IRS. Usually, Form K-1 reports an individual's share of partnership and S corporation income.

- **C corporations:** Unlike a sole proprietorship or a partnership, for federal tax purposes, a C corporation is recognized as a separate tax-paying entity. This means the corporation may take special deductions. Still, it also means the profit earned is taxed at the corporate level, then again on your individual tax return if it is distributed as a dividend.

- **S corporations:** An S corporation is similar to a partnership in that the income typically flows through to your individual tax return. But you usually set a salary, withholding payroll taxes at the corporate level for the owner (you). Some or all of your income may be reported to you on a Form W-2 at the end of the year. One advantage of being an S corporation is your ability to choose a salary, subject to reasonable guidelines. However, there can be severe ramifications if you underpay yourself when your business makes money because wages are subject to payroll taxes.

- **LLCs:** An LLC is a legal business structure. However, it is a state-level designation and not generally recognized for federal tax purposes. An LLC must be filed as a corporation, partnership, or sole proprietorship.

NEXT STEPS AND TAX PREP

During the year, you may need to file estimated taxes for your business. According to the IRS, "Individuals, including sole proprietors, partners, and S corporation shareholders, generally have to make estimated tax payments if they expect to owe tax of $1,000 or more when their return is filed. Corporations generally have to make estimated tax payments if they expect to owe tax of $500 or more when their return is filed. You may have to pay estimated tax for the current year if your tax was more than zero in the prior year. See the worksheet in Form 1040-ES, Estimated Tax for Individuals, for more details on who must pay estimated tax."

Once you understand your business structure, you can take the steps to maximize tax deductions. One of the first steps to take is to secure a tax ID number.

Tax IDs are free and can be obtained through the IRS's website, https://irs.gov/businesses/small-businesses-self-employed/employer-id-numbers. It's a good idea as a sole proprietor to get a separate tax ID number for your business to give to clients or other entities who require a W-9 form. It is also a requirement if you have employees. If you've formed a partnership or corporation, this should have been done during that process, so check with the professional who assisted you with the setup and filing for your entity.

To make life easier as a US taxpayer, keeping track of the money you earn and the money you spend should be part of your daily, or at least weekly, routine. As you prepare for this year's taxes, you may be organized, or you might need a little more time to get all your information together. If you receive royalties from a publisher (traditional or self-published), you should receive a tax form stating your earnings either by email or standard mail, depending on your selection during the time you published your work. If you haven't received those yet, write to the entity who published your work and ask for it. Usually it is a Form 1099. If you sell directly, the payment processor you use should be able to generate a report of earnings from January 1 to December 31.

Pro Tip: Don't forget, you can deduct the processing fees you pay if you sell direct and your payment processor keeps a percentage.

When filing, all your numbers will be grouped into categories. You won't have to enter specifics for most deductions as long as the amount entered ads up to the total amount of receipts. Always consult a tax professional, but a best practice is to keep all receipts for at least seven years. If you get audited, having an organized tracking system—whether it's digital or paper receipts in categorized shoe boxes—is the best way to avoid heartburn.

Pro Tip: If you don't have a system in place, using a personal finance tool like Mint.com, Quick-Books, or other financial trackers throughout 2024 can help you categorize and keep track of your business and personal income and expenses separately.

MAKE THE MOST OF TAX DEDUCTIONS

When making your list of deductions, think of all the things purchased during the year for your author business. If you can carve out a little nook in your home to dedicate solely to the business of writing, you can claim a significant home office tax deduction. It does not have to be a separate room. Something as simple as a desk in the corner of the kitchen, living room, bedroom, or other space will qualify. The stipulation is that it must be used exclusively for business tasks.

Use the list of examples below to jumpstart your tracking, but always consult with a tax professional to ensure deductions are accounted for properly:

- Office supplies
- Reference materials—include any books, fiction or nonfiction, you purchase for genre or story research
- Travel expenses
- Conference/workshop fees
- Cover designs
- Website/newsletter expenses
- Design services
- Advertising/marketing
- Promotional expenses
- Postage

- Subscriptions (KU, Audible, *IAM*, Book Brush, Canva, Adobe, etc.)
- Promotional merchandise

This list of deductible items is quite large, but meticulous bookkeeping and receipt filing is necessary to satisfy IRS rules.

In addition to income taxes, you may be required to collect and pay sales tax on physical products. Sales tax varies from state to state, so check your state's guidelines to see if you should be charging customers sales tax for your physical products like books or other merchandise. If you should have collected taxes and didn't, you can be personally liable for the sales tax you should have collected. Check with your tax professional to ensure proper filing on sales of physical products.

Finally, if you have employees on your payroll, including yourself, you and they must pay the standard payroll tax on income. We said it in the beginning, but it should be reiterated that employing the services of a tax expert matched to your unique situation is a best practice that should be part of your author business—and yes, you can deduct this year's tax prep expenses on next year's return. An expert can uncover industry-specific deductions for more tax breaks and file your taxes, giving you the peace of mind you need to continue writing and creating freely.

If you need assistance finding forms or experts to help prepare your taxes, use the links below to explore more resources.

https://irs.gov/businesses
https://turbotax.intuit.com/tax-tips
https://hrblock.com/tax-center/lifestyle/tax-tips ■

Tiffany Robinson

Tiffany Robinson

Tiffany Robinson writes contemporary romance under two different pen names because she loves the happily-ever-after. She's also a freelance content writer, writing coach, and online educator. She and her husband have been running their own business since 2010 and have two young boys who keep them on their toes. Outside of writing, running a business, and momming, her hobbies include cooking and running. She knows it's weird, but everybody's got their thing.

Gone Phishing

CYBERSECURITY TIPS TO AVOID SCAMS TARGETING YOUR AUTHOR BUSINESS

Scams became much more prevalent with the widespread use of the internet, and as perpetrators grow more sophisticated and continue to update their tactics, it's no longer just the technologically un-savvy who are falling victim. Cybersecurity professionals categorize many of these scams with the term "phishing," and these scams are sadly increasing—according to a 2023 report by Zscaler, with a year-over-year increase of nearly 50 percent.

Common email scams can target banking or retail customers—"log in or your account will be closed"—that aim to steal passwords. Other scams demand the receiver submit private data to a malicious website. In my twenty years of working in cybersecurity, I'm seeing more email scams than ever before specifically target authors and other creative businesspeople. Here are some of the latest examples—and how to recognize them.

SCAMS TARGETING YOUR LIVELIHOOD

As indie authors, we've all heard the horror stories of authors who say their Amazon or Facebook business accounts were canceled for no reason. As it's difficult to get the "real reason" behind these disappearing accounts out of the parent companies, many indie authors live in fear of this happening to them. So when emails appear stating the recipient has violated terms or service and will have their account canceled unless they respond immediately, it's natural for authors to react.

Unfortunately, many authors have fallen victim to giving their Amazon or Facebook username and password—or even payment and banking information—to the perpetrators of these scams. With your Amazon information, scammers can often access your credit card information or send tens of thousands of dollars of merchandise, with you paying for it. With your Facebook information, scammers can access your contact list, making it easier to scam your friends and family or to implement Facebook Marketplace scams under your name.

SCAMS TARGETING PAYMENT FOR YOUR WORK

Several years ago, an email "deposit-and-return" scam became popular where the scammer would try to convince a victim to send a few hundred dollars in order to receive a larger payout. Often, the scammer would tell the victim a sad story over email—often mentioning a large amount of money the scammer can't access—but promise a larger payout in return for a payment that would allow them to access the large amount of money. The larger payment never materializes.

Today, that scam has evolved into a fake purchase of creative assets. These scams generally work like this: the scammer will request licensing of an author or artist's story or artwork for several thousand dollars for a project or workshop. The payment will then be made with a cashier's check or another non-cash method. Immediately afterward, the scammer will send a communication canceling the project and will request a refund of the money. The author or artist might send back the money before the cashier's check, or other payment type, clears their bank, only to discover later that the check was fake—and they're out several thousand dollars.

Over the last few years, many authors have received scam emails from a variety of real Hollywood movie studios, literary agencies, and publishers, using the names of real employees at the business, telling the author their book has big potential for a movie, a publication deal, or something similar. The first email often simply asks for a reply. If the author replies, the scammer then sends a variety of paid offers for services to turn the book into a screenplay, a treatment, a professional synopsis—all for thousands of dollars. These scammers take the money and disappear.

HOW TO SPOT THESE SCAMS

No matter the target audience of an email scam, most of them have several of the following factors in common:

- uses a business name that is trusted, crucial to your business, or both, such as Amazon, Facebook/Meta, TriStar Pictures, or PayPal;
- expresses a sense of urgency, especially for threats to cancel your Amazon or Facebook ads accounts;
- generic greeting or non-specific references to your books;
- a "from" email address close to—but not a match—with the official business; or
- an email that invites you to click on a link to fix the issue.

Well-established companies are often victims of these scams and employ enterprise-level software solutions, often for tens or hundreds of thousands of dollars, to prevent these scam emails from reaching their users. As indie authors, we're not in a position to implement these larger security solutions, so vigilance has to be our first defense.

Therefore, experts suggest you look for the following items to minimize the risk of falling victim to one of these scams:

Look at the "from" email address. If it isn't from a domain name matching the business, there's a high probability that it's a scam. For example, "tristar-pictures-inc@gmail.com" was a scam sender in a scam email to get a movie made of an unspecified book. The company logo in the header or email isn't proof of anything genuine.

If there's a link in the email, move your mouse over the link, but do not click. After a second or two, a URL will appear—and if it's a scam, the URL will not match a real Amazon or Facebook or Paramount Pictures link.

Is there a lack of specificity? Genuine emails will never say "Dear customer" or "Dear ma'am or sir." Requests to turn your book into a movie will specify which book the company is interested in—not refer to it as "your book."

Even if the link looks real, never click on a link inside an email to enter your username and password or update your payment information. Instead, exit your email program and log in directly to your Amazon KDP account or Meta Business Suite if you are worried there's an issue.

If you receive a one-time passcode on your phone but didn't request it, do not provide it to anyone over the phone or via text.

Check it out—outside of email. Call someone at the organization (using a phone number that's NOT in the email). Search on scam-reporting sites like Writer Beware; an experience just like yours may have been identified as a scam.

OTHER SCAMS

Email scams that install malware, keyloggers, or viruses on your computer when you click on a link are common, though not usually targeted specifically at authors. Predatory "vanity publishers" will request thousands of dollars from writers in order to publish their book, then expend minimum effort in editing, cover design, and marketing. Similarly, some companies offer author-unfriendly terms for serialized fiction that leave little if any money for the author—and can lock them in for years. Although not the same as the email phishing scams described here, these bad business practices can correctly be called "scams" as well, and Writer Beware has excellent advice on recognizing and avoiding these businesses; an article summarizing 2023's biggest scams and issues is particularly impactful.

WHAT IF YOU FALL VICTIM TO A SCAM?

Time isn't your friend if you've been a victim. First, contact any financial institution that may have been affected and report possible fraud. There is a chance you may not be held responsible for fraudulent transactions, but this depends on the transaction. Change any potentially compromised passwords. If you suspect malware has been installed on your machine, disconnect or power down your device, and contact a professional who deals with malware.

If you've disclosed credit card or banking information, or potentially given scammers access to this information via a separate account, you may need to cancel your debit and credit cards, as well as freeze your credit. In the USA, you must freeze your credit with all three credit reporting agencies: Experian, Equifax, and TransUnion.

Many countries offer places to report fraud and scams. In the USA, scam emails can be reported to reportphishing@apwg.org, and victims can report to the Federal Trade Commission (https://FTC.gov/complaint).

RESOURCES

- Defining and avoiding phishing scams: https://webroot.com/us/en/resources/tips-articles/what-is-phishing
- The U.S. Federal Trade Commission's advice on avoiding online scams: https://consumer.ftc.gov/articles/how-recognize-and-avoid-phishing-scams
- The prevalence and impact of phishing attacks: https://blog.checkpoint.com/2023/01/23/brand-phishing-report-q4-2022/
- Author-specific advice and resources on avoiding scams of all kinds: https://writer-beware.blog/ ∎

Paul Austin Ardoin

Paul Austin Ardoin

Paul Austin Ardoin is the USA TODAY bestselling indie author of The Fenway Stevenson Mysteries and The Woodhead & Becker Mysteries. He holds a B.A. in creative writing from the University of California, Santa Barbara and an M.B.A. in marketing from the University of Phoenix. His book Zero to Four Figures: Making $1,000 a Month with Self-Published Fiction is scheduled for publication in June 2023.

It's a Numbers Game

K-LYTICS HELPS AUTHORS UNDERSTAND THE INDUSTRY WITH DATA-DRIVEN INSIGHTS

The average indie author has probably heard about K-lytics founder Alex Newton's monthly Amazon Kindle data deep dive. In each report, he curates aggregate data, both historical and current, and provides analytical insights into the state of things on Amazon's Kindle store.

For those with an eye for numbers, K-lytics reporting can offer a look at what readers want in your genre, as well as larger trends in the publishing industry. Give it time, and that understanding could lead to a potential boost for your books on the online storefront. Below, we'll cover key features of K-lytics reporting and what data it can provide to better assist you in making decisions for your author business.

REPORTING

For those who find numbers daunting, K-lytics aims to demystify Amazon's massive amount of open-source data, compile it, and analyze it so it can be of practical use. K-lytics's primary offerings are reports: genre reports and monthly market analysis reports, both of which are broken down into observations, top selling covers by genre, blurb analysis, and more. These reports fall under three tiers: basic reports, monthly genre reports, and premium genre reports (niche focus).

Each monthly report includes metrics such as sales volume, rank momentum, competition, effort to enter the market, and category power. K-lytics analyzes more than thirty main book genres, four hundred sub-markets and two thousand four hundred sub-sub-markets and offers a statistical analysis of how well particular categories are performing by the metric. Using K-lytics's reports, you can get valuable data, such as the average sales rank of the top twenty titles, estimated sales per day of the top twenty titles, and the average sales rank of No. 1 bestsellers.

Digging into the individual reports, genre reports are typically updated every year and include major genres such as Thriller, Sci-Fi, Fantasy, and Romance. Occasionally, a niche-specific report within the genre report will come available. These are considered deep dives into the intricacies of the genre and include more information, such as category heat maps, pricing analysis, and other vital market intelligence.

For example, Romance has a place in the monthly report. However, genres such as Mafia Romance and Fantasy Romance have emerged as popular genres; thus, K-lytics has provided updated reporting on those specific niches and subcategories. A list of K-lytics deep-dive genre reports can be found here: https://k-lytics.com/shop.

PRESENTATION

K-lytics reporting comes as a PDF document, and inside is a link to a video analysis with Newton himself guiding you through the report. A basic report includes overall sales volume information and a bar chart outlining the sales volume of the top one hundred titles from a visual perspective. Each category is numbered based on the performance index, so you can see which of the main genre categories are performing the best. For example, the report from December 2023 shows Romance is the clear category winner with an average sales rank of ninety-two for the top one hundred titles and an estimated 644 sales per day of the top selling title. There are other charts including line graphs that depict sales rank over time of the top one hundred titles, heat map charts that identify niches within genres organized by bestsellers, and word cloud charts of the most popular words found in bestseller blurbs. Each chart in the report has a specific focus meant to drive business decisions.

Pro Tip: Each report comes with a heat map showing the genres and subgenres doing well in what are considered "hot" genres. Use the heat map to quickly identify where your current books stand among similar genres.

PRICING

K-lytics offers two different pricing structures, one-offs and a subscription. The one-off purchases can be made at https://k-lytics.com/shop and include previous genre-specific reports. The cost of individual reports runs between $37 and $47 each, and each will provide you with a detailed report and video walk-through of the report itself. Each report is yours to keep forever.

To get access to the monthly reports and all other historical reports, you'll need to purchase one of three membership levels: Premium, Elite or Elite (Annual Pass), each of which has access to the same type of statistical analysis but with a substantial increase in data points analyzed. K-Lytics charges $37 per month for its lowest tier, Premium; $97 a month for Elite; or $497 for an entire year of reporting. In addition, the Elite and Elite (Annual Pass) options include data on more than 7,750 genre categories. Premium tier members have access to reports on 450 genre categories.

Pro Tip: Both Elite and Elite (Annual Pass) also boast access to VIP support from the K-lytics team to answer your questions.

Some authors may not need access to reporting on a monthly basis. If you find you don't need to receive updated reports each month, K-lytics allows members to pause their subscriptions as needed, then resume monthly payments when they're ready.

STRENGTH IN THE NUMBERS

Where K-lytics thrives is in its nonpartisan look at both current and historical data on Amazon, identifying trends and making predictions toward the future of the Amazon platform. This data is invaluable to the savvy indie author or publisher who wants to know which categories the best-selling books in the genre are picking, words commonly found across the blurbs, or the length or price of a particular book. The tool's comprehensive reports aggregate data into an easily digestible format that can be used to make swift decisions while cutting out the need for authors to do extensive research on their own.

Pro Tip: K-lytics reports often have a list of the top one hundred books in a given category or genre depending on the book. Each listed book has a direct link to the Amazon page, where you can view the book itself.

Where K-lytics falls behind is in its narrow focus on Amazon KDP. The reports do not have a similar counterpart to those who are "wide" or "direct," or for those selling audiobooks. Authors who do not publish through KDP, or authors who want to understand sales trends on other platforms, will need to find other tools and services with equivalent information that applies to their business model.

WHO WOULD BENEFIT MOST?

From the average author planning their second series to those looking to break into a new genre, K-lytics is an excellent tool to get a snapshot of the market before you invest valuable time and creative energy into it. If you are using Amazon as a distributor and market for your books in any regard, you are the type of author most likely to benefit from the knowledge available from K-lytics.

If writing to market is part of your business model, K-lytics reports show what the average market has decided is current by heat-indexing popular categories and subcategories, or by providing word clouds of the top blurbs that are moving a lot of books daily.

Finally, if you simply want to know how a market is doing overall on a monthly historical basis, K-lytics can provide you with aggregate data and a view of the industry as a whole, so you can be a well-informed business owner. ■

David Viergutz

David Viergutz

David Viergutz is a disabled Army Veteran, Law Enforcement Veteran, husband and proud father. He is an author of stories from every flavor of horror and dark fiction. One day, David's wife sat him down and gave him the confidence to start putting his imagination on paper. From then on out his creativity has no longer been stifled by self-doubt and he continues to write with a smile on his face in a dark, candle-lit room.

From the Stacks

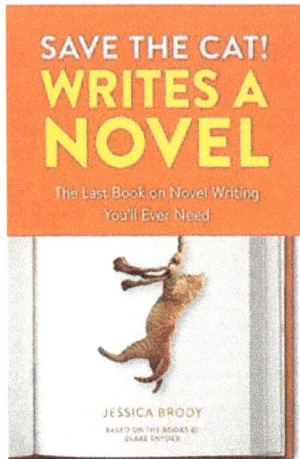

Save the Cat! Writes a Novel
https://indieauthortools.com/books/
save-the-cat-writes-a-novel
Written by Jessica Brody, *Save the Cat! Writes a Novel* combines the renowned screen-writing methodology of *Save the Cat!* with a novelist's template to a compelling story. Using a fifteen-plot-point framework and identifying ten specific story genres, this novel belongs in a novelist's toolbox for plot and story structure.

Pabbly Connect
https://pabbly.com/connect/
In a time of connectivity, nothing is more frustrating than an application that lacks the necessary integration to connect with your other technology. Pabbly Connect markets itself as a Zapier alternative, capable of automations, integration, and task management. Pabbly Connect works with software such as MailerLite and KingSumo to automate tasks that would otherwise steal your valuable time.

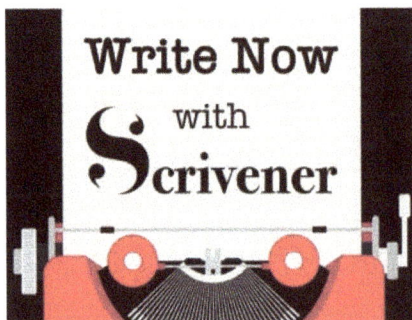

Write Now with Scrivener
https://podcast.scrivenerapp.com/
Guided by journalist Kirk McElhearn, *Write Now with Scrivener* is a podcast dedicated to interviewing writers of every flavor about their processes and techniques, and exploring how they use Scrivener to aid those processes. The first half of each show is dedicated to the writer's approach and process. The second half shows how Scrivener is incorporated into the writer's workflow.

How Fanfiction Can Reignite an Author's Passion

Many years ago, I developed a desire to read more classics, so I thought about trying Jane Austen's works. I had never read her books, but I'd seen a movie or two and enjoyed the stories. The only book available from the library without a month's waitlist was *Persuasion*. After I read the book, I fell in love with the characters and the world Austen had created. I ended up reading all her books, but I still wanted more. I could not get enough of Anne Elliot and Captain Wentworth.

Then I discovered fanfiction. There was a trove of stories about these treasured characters I could enjoy beyond Austen's original work. There were eighty-seven fanfictions on Fanfiction.net about *Persuasion*. I read every single one of them. I'm sure there are many more to be found now.

It was still not enough. Ideas of where I would have preferred the characters to go danced in mind and would not let me go. I ended up writing a fanfiction novel based on the book. Because Austen's work was over two hundred years old and out of copyright, unlike most fanfiction authors, I could publish my book freely. As a first-time author, Austen's name recognition boosted my sales beyond my expectations.

WHAT IS FANFICTION?

Fanfiction is a vibrant literary subculture where enthusiasts delve into established fictional universes, crafting their own stories based on existing characters and settings. It's derivative work that allows new authors to explore alternate plotlines, character relationships, or events within the confines of their favorite books, movies, TV shows, and other media. Even retellings of fairy tales are fair game. Writers engage in fanfiction to express their love for a particular narrative, often adding depth to underdeveloped secondary characters or exploring hypothetical scenarios. It often features a strong LGTBQ+ representation, written by their community for their community and the world at large.

The community thrives on a sense of camaraderie, feedback, and shared passion for the source material, fostering a unique space for writers to experiment and hone their craft. The lure of using someone else's world-building and characters, leaving the author to work on plots alone, can help a budding storyteller find their footing. However, the practice isn't just for those who are beginner storytellers.

WHY WOULD A PUBLISHED AUTHOR CARE ABOUT FANFICTION?

For published authors, delving into the world of fanfiction can be liberating. It offers a unique platform to engage directly with a passionate fanbase, creating an avenue for further connection and dialogue. By encouraging others to write fanfiction of their works, authors empower readers to become participants in the storytelling process, breathing new life into familiar characters and settings and becoming a source of promotion for their original books.

The feedback loop with fanfiction readers can provide insights into what resonates with your audience, helping you understand diverse interpretations of your work. Ultimately, embracing fanfiction can be a symbiotic relationship, fostering a dynamic exchange between creators and their devoted community.

Sometimes, a published author is the fan themself. Writing fanfiction of other author's universes can be a palate cleanser, and while you cannot always publish the work of another for pay, you could still find readers for your author brand on fanfiction platforms. The fanfiction readers who enjoy your depictions of other author's work could move on to your regular offerings.

The fanfiction genre doesn't have to be just a fun writing exercise for beginning storytellers; whether as a low-stakes writing exercise or an unconventional marketing tactic, it can also be a worthwhile corner of the community for established authors to explore.

WHERE TO FIND FANFICTION

Archive of Our Own
https://archiveofourown.org
A favored platform for fanfiction, Archive of Our Own, also known as AO3, includes writing from both amateur and professional writers. The search engine is efficient and user-friendly.

Fanfiction.net
https://fanfiction.net
This is the largest fanfiction archive and forum. Their website features quality writing and a vast assortment of universes to choose from, which you can find via search or a well-organized folder system.

Wattpad
https://wattpad.com/stories/fanfiction
One of the better-known fanfiction platforms, Wattpad has a large selection of original content and fanfictions. Most of the work is geared toward young adult audiences.

DeviantArt
https://deviantart.com/search?q=fanfiction
More known for being an online art community of painters, illustrators, and photographers, DeviantArt also hosts a vibrant community of writers. You can find original stories, poetry, and fanfiction.

LEXICON OF TERMS RELATED TO FANFICTION

Beyond the typical trope names and genre trends that exist in most genre fiction, the fanfiction community has created many of its own terms, which could be confusing to a new reader. Below are explanations for some of the more common ones.

Angst: Emotional distress is a key element in angst-labeled fanfiction, where a significant emphasis is placed on portraying the profound unhappiness experienced by the characters.

AU: Alternate universe; describes a narrative that deviates significantly, often involving major changes to the plot, setting, or characters, diverging from the established canon.

Bashing: Describes a phenomenon where an author harboring dislike for a character or pairing manifests their aversion within the story by showcasing disdain for the character or pairing.

Canon: The foundational material from which fanfiction draws its inspiration. Any element existing in the original source material is part of the canon or is described as canonical.

Crossover: A fusion of various canonical sources.

Fan Service: Denotes scenes within the original canon source material intentionally crafted as nods to the fanbase. These may include in-jokes or bonus scenes designed for fans to recognize, catering specifically to them, rather than the broader viewer audience.

Feels: The powerful emotions evoked in readers by specific scenes or character developments within a story or canon, eliciting intense emotional responses.

Femslash: From female and slash; a fiction that explores a romantic or sexual connection between characters, both of whom are female.

Fluff: Charming, low-drama fanfiction, frequently centered on romance.

HEA: Happily ever after; describes narratives where characters experience romantic relationships culminating in a permanent pairing.

Het: Heterosexual; this type of fanfiction centers on a romantic or sexual relationship between a male and a female character.

H/C: Hurt/comfort; a fanfiction where a character undergoes suffering and is subsequently comforted or assisted in their recovery by other characters.

Idfic: Self-indulgent fanfiction. The term "idfic" is typically employed as a self-aware acknowledgment rather than as a criticism.

Lurker: Describes a reader who refrains from providing comments or reviews on a fiction or post.

Podfic: Describes a type of transformative work where fanfiction stories are presented in audio form through the podcast format.

Profic: Describes entirely original stories crafted with professional writing standards and published to generate profit. Many authors, who initially embark on their writing journeys through fanfiction before transitioning to professional realms, opt to remove any unauthorized fanfics from the internet upon achieving success to avoid potential copyright infringement issues.

Shipper: Describes an individual who advocates for the concept of two particular characters engaging in a romantic or sexual relationship.

Slash: Denotes the inclusion of a same-sex relationship involving at least one established canon character. It may or may not encompass explicit sexual content. The term is derived from the "/" symbol used to signify the specific characters paired together, originating from the Kirk/Spock (*Star Trek*) slash pairing over four decades ago. Male/male homosexual content is universally referred to as "slash." ∎

Wendy Van Camp

Wendy Van Camp

Wendy Van Camp is the Poet Laureate for the City of Anaheim, California. Her work is influenced by cutting edge technology, astronomy, and daydreams. A graduate of the Ad Astra Speculative Fiction Workshop, Wendy is a nominated finalist for the Elgin Award, for the Pushcart Prize, and for a Dwarf Stars Award. Her poems, stories, and articles have appeared in: "Starlight Scifaiku Review", "The Junction", "Quantum Visions", and other literary journals. She is the poet and illustrator of "The Planets: a scifaiku poetry collection" and editor of the annual anthology "Eccentric Orbits: An Anthology of Science Fiction Poetry". Find her at https://wendyvancamp.com

See Your Goals Beyond the Murky Middle

If you're like me, by February, the newness of the year has worn off and with it a smidge of your enthusiasm. It's not that I'm not still excited about the goals I set back in December or the action items I devised in order to achieve them.

It's simply that we've now entered what I affectionately like to call "the ugly middle." Yes, I borrowed a writing phrase to describe the months of February through October. Willpower is gone, and it must be replaced with … well, what, exactly?

A CLEAR PICTURE OF THE END

Going into 2023, I had a list of seven books to write. Did I write them all? Yes, and I even published them. But it wasn't much past this time that I was questioning my choices. *Was I biting off more than I could chew? Should I revamp my goals, publication calendar, and writing schedule?*

I had to stay focused on two things: what I had decided to do, and why I had decided that in the first place.

The "what" was easy: the list of books, broken down into a daily word count goal, fit into my morning writing time. Write an average of six hundred words per day, five or six days a week, and I'd systematically write each manuscript. Easy, right? Not so fast.

It didn't take long for the challenges and roadblocks to show up, which is when I had to circle back to my "why."

Why #1: A few of the books had been on my list for far too long. They were past due. I'd been talking about writing them, thinking about writing them, and as anyone could see, they were not published.

Why #2: Some bigger, long-term goals relied upon those books' completion. Can't move on until they're done.

Why #3: I wanted to prove to myself I could do it, regardless of challenges and roadblocks, no matter what else was going on. If I was encouraging others to write amid "all the things," I needed to speak from experience, not theory.

When I fell behind later in the year, my editor asked if I was going to turn in manuscript number six on time. I lied and said, "Yes! We are all good." Then I had to move heaven and earth—well, myself and my fingers—to make that deadline. But I did it.

Why am I sharing this with you?

There are a few reasons, but the main one is this: by the time you read this, the bloom may well be off of the new year's rose. In order to find out what you're made of, and achieve the goals you set for yourself back when the eggnog was flowing and everything was jolly and bright, you must hold not just the goal but your vision in mind.

It might be easy for you to recall your goals. In fact, I hope it is! Before you blink and it's too far into the year for you to achieve them, sit down and write a clear vision of what your life and writing business will be like at the end of the year … when you've achieved your goals.

I used to write my goals in my journal and review them the next time I set goals (oops). Unsurprisingly, this was highly ineffective. Now, I write each of my goals—I set five total for the year—on a brightly colored note card and put it on my bathroom mirror. I can't miss them; in fact, I see them several times a day, starting bright and early every morning. I've done this for a few years now, and I've been hitting my goals earlier and easier than ever.

Dig out your goals and put them on your bathroom mirror, on your refrigerator, and even on the sun visor in your car. Every time you see them, recommit to achieving them by taking consistent daily action, and you will do it!

Happy writing! ∎

Honorée Corder

Honorée Corder

Honorée Corder is the author of more than fifty books, an empire builder, and encourager of writers. When she's not writing, she's spoiling her dog and two cats, eating something fabulous her husband made on the grill, working out, or reading. She hopes this article made a positive impact on your life, and if it did, you'll reach out to her via HonoreeCorder.com.

Creative Couplings

FOR THREE AUTHORS AND THEIR PARTNERS, A WRITING CAREER OFFERS A CHANCE TO SHOW THEY CARE

In the solitary world of indie authorship, where the journey of crafting words into stories is often a lone endeavor, the role of a supportive partner becomes immeasurably valuable. Beyond the quiet hours spent typing away at keyboards and wrestling with plot lines lies the crucial yet often unseen support system provided by spouses or partners.

This month, *IAM* spoke to three couples about how this support manifests in their lives and what it means to them. Whether their partners supported their work simply by being present, by managing part of the business, or as an indie author themselves, each couple shared their experience of creating a foundation from which literary dreams can soar.

AUTHOR HM HODGSON AND HER HUSBAND, HENRY EPSTEIN

Henry: I believe in people chasing their dreams. Heather supported me when I was a touring golf professional traveling the world chasing my dream, and now it's her time to shine. Heather is obsessed with her work, and it's her drive that motivates me to want to do better. Five a.m. starts, strategy sessions, writing everywhere and anywhere. I love watching her work constantly adapting and learning. My job is simple—bring the woman her coffee and watch her go to work.

Heather: Two years ago, when I wanted to quit my day job and turn my passion into a permanent career change, Henry said do it. He's also helped with some of the best plot twists in the stories themselves. Maybe because we're total opposites, he sees opportunities in stories that I haven't considered. And while we have our differences, we also both love Action and Adventure movies with plenty of romance—don't tell him that—so he gets what I'm trying to achieve with my books. Plus, he brings me coffee and writing snacks. The man's a keeper.

AUTHOR KAT T MASEN AND HER HUSBAND AND BUSINESS PARTNER, STEVE TERAN

Kat: In 2021, Steve quit his full-time job to support my author career. From that moment, it was no longer my author career but our business and newly founded company, Masen Ink. With Steve on board, we grew to a seven-figure company within one year. His dedication to learning about the book world is ongoing, and now, three years later, he is head of our operations. Working together as a married couple with four children is challenging. Still, we make an effort to sit down regularly and map out goals, so we both understand what is needed to continue growing our company.

Steve: Working in a different industry proved to be challenging at the beginning. The book world is nothing like the corporate role I'd been in for over twenty years. The key to working together is to recognize each other's strengths. I'm not one for social media and strive in operations and logistics. Kat is all social media with strong skills in marketing. She has a creative personality and is constantly pushing the boundaries with her ideas and eagerness to grow.

AUTHORS AND SPOUSES BEN WOLF AND CHARIS CROWE

Ben: Charis's primary support for me over the years has been her belief in me. She has never wavered in her belief that I could accomplish my goals, even if it didn't happen right away. The pros of us being authors are that we both understand this business and what it takes to make headway in a challenging industry. The cons are that we sometimes have different expectations of each other when it comes to workflow, so we occasionally have to resolve conflicts along those lines.

Charis: One of the biggest ways Ben supports me is through his versatility. We've both been in the writing industry for fifteen-plus years, and during that time, Ben has worn many more writing-related-profession hats than I have: editor, publisher, author, writing coach, print broker, and salesman, just to name a few. The pros of being married to another author? He always "gets it." I never have to explain the mechanics of whatever I'm going through. If I hit a wall with a plot, he can talk me through it. If we need to order out for dinner or change our plans because I'm on a roll writing, he understands and prioritizes my work. As for the cons—when you both work from home, the dishes pile up a lot faster. ◼

Tanya Nellestein

Tanya Nellestein

Tanya Nellestein is an avid reader, experience enthusiast, outstanding car vocalist, and Queen of fancy dress. In her spare time she is also a bestselling and award-winning author and journalist with a penchant for bloodthirsty battles and steamy romance. From Vikings to present day, Tanya writes page-turning, gut-churning stories with a romantic angle that always includes good sex and a happily ever after - eventually. Her debut novel, The Valkyrie's Viking recently hit Amazon's best seller list and her sixth novel, This Side of Fate, was the 2022 winner of the Romance Writers of Australia Sapphire Award for Best Unpublished Romance Manuscript. In 2021, Tanya won the Romance Writers of Australia Romance in Media Award. Tanya lives on the outskirts of Sydney, Australia amidst a cavalcade of never ending disasters, both natural and those of her own making.

The Dreaded Blurb

Writing a book's blurb is one of the first steps in book marketing and one authors love to lament. You have to boil your entire book down into a few punchy lines that will entice the reader without giving away the story and somehow leave them with a desperate need to know more.

The amazing cover you love so much will entice a reader to explore the blurb, but it is the blurb that truly sells the book.

So how do you do it?

There are several strategies authors use, but I want to share mine with you. When I write my book's blurbs, I break the task down into sections and always start with an opening hook: a single line that is intended to spike their interest. For my first book, I wrote, "Fight a demon, investigate a werewolf biker gang, have tea with mum…it's all in a day's work for England's #1 paranormal P.J."

In twenty-three words, I introduced genre tropes—demon, werewolf—showed that the subject matter is probably lighthearted since he is going to have tea with his mum, and made it clear this is a story about a paranormal investigator in England.

Here are a couple more examples of one-line introductions. The first is just thirteen words, and it hits the ball out of the park: "When my magic manifested at puberty, my parents sold me to the Illuminati."

The central character has a backstory I already need to know more about. What's more, I know she has magic she can employ, but how strong is she? Did she escape from the Illuminati?

Here is another one, taken from a recent Amazon.com bestseller.

"'Welcome to the family,' Nina Winchester says as I shake her elegant, manicured hand. I smile

Paranormal Nonsense: Blue Moon Investigations Book 1 - A Supernatural Thriller Kindle Edition

by Steve Higgs (Author)   Format: Kindle Edition

4.2 ★★★★☆ ˅   3,641 ratings   4.0 on Goodreads 2,615 ratings

Book 1 of 22: Blue Moon Investigations

See all formats and editions

Kindle from $5.99	Hardcover $17.99	Paperback $13.24
Read with our **free** app	1 New from $17.99	3 Used from $13.20 1 New from $13.24

Fight a demon, investigate a werewolf biker gang, have tea with mum … it's all in a day's work for England's #1 paranormal P.I.

politely, gazing around the marble hallway. Working here is my last chance to start fresh. I can pretend to be whoever I like. But I'll soon learn that the Winchesters' secrets are far more dangerous than my own …'"

Dangerous secrets, hints of a past yet to be revealed, and the need to know more. Why is she being welcomed into the family?

Of course, you want to perfect the opening line, but then you must tell the reader a little more. Introduce your main character(s) and give them dimension. Talk about the dilemma your characters are facing, and aim to give your reader a reason to care or be interested enough to find out more:

"In 1938, a small crooked-legged racehorse received more press coverage than Hitler, Mussolini, Roosevelt or any other news figure." The reader now needs to know why.

"In 1944, British bomber pilot Hugo Langley parachuted from his stricken plane into the verdant fields of German-occupied Tuscany. Badly wounded, he found refuge in a ruined monastery and in the arms of Sofia Bartoli. But the love that kindled between them was shaken by an irreversible betrayal." What betrayal?

Once you have created intrigue, it's time to stop and leave potential readers wanting more. Finishing the blurb with a cliff-hanger is one strategy employed brilliantly in the following example: "Joanna soon discovers that some would prefer the past be left undisturbed, but she has come too far to let go of her father's secrets now …"

The final element I have yet to mention is the review quote.

Traditionally published novels often include review quotes in their blurbs, and you should too. I place mine in italics and sometimes use it as the opening line. Here are two examples from my books:

"It's like Jack Reacher got stuck inside an episode of Scooby-Doo and chose to punch his way out!"

"When Steve Higgs writes, he hits it out of the park. I find myself laughing out loud and often."

These are a way to tell the reader more, compare your work to that of other authors they may be more familiar with, and give them one more reason to make that purchase.

Writing a blurb is very different from writing a book in many ways, but if you don't get it right, it can be the difference between selling one copy a week and ten copies a day. The good news is that you can try different things out, swapping the opening lines, your review quotes, or the whole thing until you have one that works.

Good luck! ∎

Steve Higgs

Steve Higgs

High school Valedictorian enlists in the Marine Corps under a guaranteed tank contract. An inauspicious start that was quickly superseded by excelling in language study.

YOUR ONE-STOP RESOURCE

INDIE AUTHOR TOOLS

📚 Over 45+ categories of resources, from AI to website builders, all designed to supercharge your self-publishing journey.

✍️ Authentic reviews and real-world case studies from authors who've used these tools to bring their creative visions to life.

♟️ A community-powered project, crowdsourced by authors who know exactly what you need because they've been there too!

🚀 Boost your authorial prowess with our popular weekly newsletter, packed with tips, tricks, and updates on the latest tools.

www.ingramcontent.com/pod-product-compliance
Lightning Source LLC
Chambersburg PA
CBHW042342030426
42335CB00030B/3435